WEATHERED

By the same author:

Poetry:

The Flaw in the Pattern
The Quiet Blue World
The Sixth Creek
Sliding down the belly of the world

Fiction:

The Art of Breaking Ice
The Application of Pressure

WEATHERED

RACHAEL MEAD

RECENT
WORK
PRESS

Weathered
Recent Work Press
Canberra, Australia

Copyright © Rachael Mead, 2024

ISBN: 9780645973273 (paperback)

 A catalogue record for this
book is available from the
NATIONAL
LIBRARY   National Library of Australia
OF AUSTRALIA

Cover image: 'the clouds looking somewhat ominous' by Andy Melton, 2007,
reproduced under Creative Commons licence 2.0
Cover design: Recent Work Press
Set by Recent Work Press

recentworkpress.com

PL

for Andrew and Ron

Contents

I

TRAVELLING WITH THE WRONG MAP

II

CHLOROPHYLL & CASEIN

III

CONTACT TRACING

'Climate is what we expect, weather is what we get.'
Robert A. Heinlein, *Time Enough for Love.*

'Crying came out of her like weather.'
Ali Smith, *Autumn.*

I

TRAVELLING WITH THE WRONG MAP

'The world, the real is not an object. It is a process.'
John Cage

Directions to the end of the day

Let the screen door to the shearers' kitchen slap shut
on the stove-top's curls of steam and, heart throbbing
with the day's caffeine, set your course for silence and air.

Leave conversation at your back and take the dirt road
to the windmill, then turn toward the hard edge of winter
letting the south wind muscle through your clothes.

The country roars, air pushing itself into your ears
so let the wind snarl in the trap of your hair and pull
your thoughts home from their adventures. Remember,

the opposite of attention isn't distraction, it's neglect.
In this grainy hour it all becomes clear—this place
asks both hardness and humility. Push yourself uphill,

cheekbones slicing the cold, past beards of lichen and litterings
of scats, breath huffing in round vowels and feet beating the need
for space into red dust. Life may be short, but desire? Desire is long.

Keep moving but stay in the heart of your own sound—
the swoosh of jean and jacket, the clomp of boot on rock,
the heartbeat of your limp. Trust the wisdom of goats

until you struggle out of shadow onto the hill's spine,
emptiness unfolding in all directions. Breathe,
as the low sun pours its sheaves across the range,

and when you feel the boundary between your skin
and the world begin to blur, let your heart inhale,
your voice a drift of pollen. Feel the crush of layers

in the rock beneath your feet, this mass of stone
that underpins us creating its own rules of geometry
and beauty. Read the land's thirsty script,

the piles of strata built and broken over aeons
hold a narrative that tells of everything
that's laid bare and all that endures unseen.

Rest in the cradle of surplus light and rising dark,
this hillside a ghost of the one you climbed.
Set your compass for the pole star of campfire.

The night is a clean darkness under a shatter
of stars, their light racing to you for millennia
in a loneliness that feels hermetically sealed.

Peel away from this silence that's the blend
of all the quiet species breathing and slip back
into your public skin. Find your place by the fire,

and as the ancients slip their ghosts into the gloves
of your fingers, watch the brindled greyhound
step softly on her way and not look back.

Horseshoe Bay

I love this place the way a dog loves its human,
wordlessly and to the bone. The shark-spotter
unzips the long, high blue and the sea is so clear
I float in green light over the dark weight of empty.

I walk the slate path to Knights Beach,
three feet taller and not needing anyone's hand,
past the Norfolk pines for the white war dead
and my old new house that I'll never own.

I've known this place since my skin was fresh
as the sand after a wave. Now I'm creased
and coarse as the granites. I feel its moods,
the pilot-light glimmer of hope for dolphins,

how everything tastes better when you're coated
in its salt. I was dumped here, tumbled breathless,
first by waves and later, a man—heart and faith
battered, learning the sea and love are fickle

and the brutal shock of metaphor. Now, my days
here are bright and free as January strains
to turn sand into glass. Sweet shade and granite,
grass and ants, prams and dogs, the sky and sea

so blue from the vast blackness behind them.
I started this poem with Whizz Fizz
and a Historic Port Elliot pennant. It closes
with chilli squid and a cold glass of white.

Long ago, this bay was forest, these granites spat
from volcanoes. The spirits of so many hover, mine
just one ghost world in the throng. This is how it happens.
Everything will be different, everything will be the same.

Beaufort Scale for internal weather

0. Sunlight hits mirrors with direct honesty. Words lie exactly where they were left, ready to snap into bright sentences. Sleep welcomes and releases with the soft precision of the tide.
1. Skin tightens into scales; not armour but a thickening that gleams, absorbing light and heat for those minutes when clouds obscure the sun. Silence and sleep are delightful as fur.
2. Light breeze is the first sign of barometric change, yet this weather feels romantic. Even the wind is poetry. The air is clean and familiar but inland the leaves are rustling.
3. The draught is gentle but rising, leaves now in constant motion. Thoughts are scattered and sentences crackle with static. White space on the page permits quiet insurrections.
4. This is still manageable. Coffee cups or wineglasses are always in reach as the wind raises dust and flurries papers. Offshore, anxieties form whitecaps.
5. A fresh breeze implies cleanliness and health. This is inaccurate. Lists blow away and life feels cluttered with the flotsam of others' decisions. Words spray and sleep sways to a rhythm that is hard to keep.
6. Waves build and break in relentless sets. There's whistling in the wires and the sun is constantly behind clouds, so who is to say when it passes the yardarm? The phone rings out. The inbox fills. Sleep is tangled in the looping playback of regret.
7. Every direction is headwind. There is only the bed, the couch and the weight of deadlines. Dark energy drives every process. Strange, unsettling thoughts blink on like stars, sharp and old. Sleep is a fox.
8. The golden age is always in the past. Everything is edge and squall, words streaking the air like dirty foam. All relationships are pacts with grief. The sky is low, pressure high. To leave the house is to risk damage.
9. The weight of air takes on the heft of the universe. The dark seethes with anxieties and sleep is far too kind for the cynicism of night. Communication lines are down. Chimneys and roofs are threatened. To venture out is unthinkable.

10. The world can only be read in translation. All trees not uprooted are potential targets. Sharp edges gleam with promise. Moon-shaped hollows are carved beneath eyes. This was all decided years ago.
11. Thoughts shake out their wildness like savages, as if the magic of facts can hold back the tides, the gales, the wars. Self-medication. Self-harm. Words are expletives targeted at the body. Everything beautiful is far away, so distant it's invisible.
12. Widespread structural damage. Zero visibility. This is the point of collapse, the black hole. Yet there's a calm that only now feels as if it's always been here. A pure, deep truth waiting to be unearthed like a fossilized bone. Here, in the centre, it is clear and still. It is up to you.

Catastrophic Fire Danger: level 6

These days are the worst kind of extraordinary, blunt
as mirrors. It's not the heat, it's the wind. Ruthless
air scrapes the house, honing itself as it passes.

Tubs are stacked by the door: passports, poetry,
our history glued in albums. The Dig Tree leaf Andrew
gave me our first week. Frames hold flares of light.

January reels beyond the glass. I prime the pumps.
I'm climate clickbait, peering out from inside the news.
I scan the blue for smoke. Plants, words, thoughts

all crackle to dust in this catastrophic light.
The axis of the earth shifts, these ranges now
the centre of the world. Leaves glare like blades.

This day is bloated with tea, dread and tedium
— as long as a life. The throb of old losses
fades. I fear only what can still be lost.

Green aches in the light. I skim the edges of air
like ticking my thumb over the plastic comfort
of a rosary. Then, at last, that gleaming hour

when verandah posts and perennials are webbed
with alien beauty. Trees and house sink in clotted
shadow while the troposphere is empty with blue.

Birds are scraps of ash, circling in hot plumes of sky.
Standing in my sweat, I dream of drizzle and overcoats,
a slow shuffle of waves, the chill, mineral gaze of stars.

281 Rundle Street, Adelaide

The dawn air brims with coffee, stale beer
and freshly washed bitumen. I step through
the veil between this world and memory
and the street is heady with cabbage, chaff
and the jostling wafts of exhaust and compost.

From The Stag, past Lemongrass to Eros Kafé,
beneath the stomp of my stride, I can hear
the grumble of Bedford flat-beds, men's laughter
and the clang of grocers' trollies echoing under
that vast iron roof while the morning dark hovers
at the Market's edges. On this stretch of footpath,
my hand always feels naked. It should be held.

A callused palm means safety. But history is vapour.
My aunt insists that Silbert, Sharp & Bishop,
where Grandpa worked for forty years, was on the right
of Frank's Lane. But I remember tripping across
that great steel plate in my shiny red shoes,
his workmates chuckling when the needle
of the huge commercial scale barely flinched.
I was sure it was the left. I'm wrong.

It's La Taberna now. Only yesterday
it was Cocolat. And just a blink before that,
I dug beneath it all as an archaeologist,
wincing every time my boss said *colonial slum.*
She sent me to dig the greasy black mire
of the tannery where, in my filthy overalls,
I unearthed a toy horse, then, hours later, its rider.

Reuniting those tiny friends thrilled the child in me,
that same excited girl whose hand Grandpa
would hold tight through the Parkland's
storybook dark as he led me to the bright clamour
of the East End Market, where strange languages
puffed in tiny clouds and men, cabled and scratchy
in hand-knitted wool, would pinch my cheeks rosier
than a Red Delicious. *Bella bambina! Ómorfo koritsáki!*

My pinafore pockets bulged with their gifts. Apples.
Peaches. As the world beyond the trucks and traders
found its daytime shape and the pigeons snuggling
on the great roof joists flapped themselves awake,
Grandpa would lead me down Rundle Street, dawn light
flushing gutters clotted with cabbage and carrot top.

In the fogged warmth of Ruby's Café, the adventure
closed with toasted sandwiches and lace-trimmed socks
swinging on the chrome stool while we waited
for the beep of Grandma's Cortina. Tucked beneath
her soft arm I'd be asleep before the last grand gum
of the Parklands ghosted my window.

Now, my worn boots stride past Gorman, Bauhaus
and M.J. Bale, where the perfume of wealth masks
the whiff of tanning pit. At Frome, I wait at the lights.
By the Austral, memory's breath of cabbage dissolves, but not
that ache to once more feel his hardened hand hold mine.

Summer 1978

after Alison Flett

chlorine and filtergulp
toes grubwhite rawpad
slapstep on pebbleedge
hotskin coldskin dive

drygrass and prickleburr
cousinshriek knifesharp
can'tswim uncle shallowend
pooledge jesuschrist

bodybrown and slipperyseal
diplegs kink bubbleblue
tongue hotchip saltburn
iceblock orangesmile

sisterpink and babyoil
hollowcheek mum cigdrag
wobblehouse on watershine
mozziepot flameflinch

brutalblue and heavyheat
auntgossip smokecurl
last simple summerjoy
toosoon skinfret bodygrief

1983

The year Han Solo was released from carbonite
I slept with my softball glove under the mattress
moulding stiff leather around that fist-hard ball,
trying to soften awkwardness into pliancy.
12 turning 13. *A Total Eclipse of the Heart*
and body. Hitting rewind on *Return of the Jedi*
until the forests of Endor stretched into static
and low-balling the pull of the Dark Side
when hormones and high school were in play.
Mandy Moffitt dumped me for the cool girls.
Bury your feelings deep down, Luke.
Lake Vostok in Antarctica hit − 89.2
but those shoulders were colder. So far
from the sun that Pioneer 10 could've
filmed me on its way past Neptune.
Keep your distance Chewie, but don't
look like you're keeping your distance.
Neither physics nor philosophy explained
how judgement could be sharp and blunt
in the same moment. My labels read *Target*
not *Sportsgirl*. Straight As meant nothing when
my other vowels sang in a working-class key.
Amo, amas, amat, amamis, amatis, amant.
Let the hate flow through you. My galaxy
was small. Conformity and authority exerted
potent gravity. *The Force is strong in my family*
meant something else entirely. I played softball.
Netball. Jumped high, long and triple. *Red Leader,*
standing by. The ultimate *Sportsgirl*. Yet those
automatic doors didn't even sense my presence.
What I told you was true, from a certain point of view.
I sang along with Boy George, dreaming of a world

that embraced more than *Colour By Numbers*.
Blue mascara and a Swatch. The tractor beam
of the mirror. *It's a trap.* I thought I needed
to be Leia. Strangle my oppressors
with my own chains. What I really needed
was to use my own eyes. Face the mirror. Say
I love you. And see my reflection mouth—*I know.*
Young fool, only now, at the end, do you understand.

My brother's heart

'Step' kept him at arm's length.
He was a flash of gold wire. I remember
playing Falklands War. From the doorway,
he'd hurl his munitions: stuffed bears,
staplers, rulers. Crouched in my trench
between bed and desk, I'd lob mine back:
plush hippo and that giant eraser I got for Christmas.
He called it 'The Mortar.' We wore bruises like medals.
He spent hours at his desk pooled in golden light,
sketching Sea Hawks and Harriers, bedroom walls
plastered with posters. Australian Test teams,
grins under the baggy green. He knew all
their batting averages with his gatling gun
spatter of stats. Cricket ball kisses
on bat and pads. We suffered each other's initiations
but failed to form a club. His room pulsed
with The Police and Dire Straits while I dreamed
of George Michael, sang 'Karma Chameleon'
into my hairbrush. Divided by more than plasterboard.
More than blood. I remember his first heart attack.
Him lying there, middle-aged in a row of old men,
shadow-eyed but trying to make light of it.
His laugh, ageless in the face of decades,
all of us sallow-skinned under ICU lights.
I remember sandy hair, toffee eyes, his bike
of gold with handlebars curled like horns.
Jason riding the golden ram. I never thought
about his heart. About all the things sliding
about in his body's dark, knowing their role.
Until now. His love beats loud in the chests
of his sons. I used to think of our childhood
as one long wait in a terminal, ready to leap

on the first bus out. Now here we are,
back in that disinfectant fug, waiting,
the taste of metal in our mouths knowing
someone must die for him to survive.

Terra incognita

On the map of who I am, this is the ripped edge:
dragons, sea-beasts, a rented car outside his house.

Roses and natives. Red brick. Tight chest.
Can't meet my eyes in the mirror.
Heels on driveway. New 4WD.
Blue door. Plain. Electrified gut. My finger on the bell.

A woman opens the door. Thickset. Short.
Silver hair. Pale eyes.   Pale.
I was wondering if I could speak with Peter Chant?
He knew my family in the late 60s.
I hand her the photo, folded so he takes up the whole frame
my mother, her shiny beehive and smile, tucked inside.
What's this about?
Cream skivvy. Lavender tunic. Clean nails.
I need to say it to him, first. The words. You're my father.

I'd just like to speak with him. Please.
So polite. So needy.
Do you have a number where he can contact you?
Scrabble in my bag. *You'd think I'd be more organised.* Yes, I say that.
I hand her my card. She closes the door.
Thank you. Blue door. Plain.
She still has the photo.

The car. Sunshine. Gulps of breath.
Cottesloe. Indian Ocean. Sea-beasts and bare feet.
The waves are glassy, then turbid. This is not my ocean.

My world compresses to ten carpeted paces.
Hotel window to peephole periscope. At the heart of the map
my phone's black screen marking what could be treasure,
or beast from the deep.

Three days. Phone fully charged.
Pillow nest. Vikings binge. Mini-bar.
Boarding pass.

A personal map of Our Nation's Capital

I

My days are national. Here, behind each façade
acknowledgements of country drone
alongside directions to toilets and exits.
White history is grass-deep, Burley Griffin's
deft designs unrolled across a stolen table.
On the Grand Axis every flag is pinned to the wind.
Old Parliament House gleams like cleaned bone
and the tent embassy clings to the lawn, flag fixed
at half-mast. I cross the National Rose Garden.
Everything is ready, claret leaves like old blood
and buds clenched and raised into fists.

II

I navigate the Deco maze of my hotel
by Prime Ministers. It's tricky. Self-important
old white men all tend to look the same.
Past Chifley, up the stairs at Holt. 'Always
turn left at Menzies' is easy to remember.

III

The National Library is seven archive boxes shelved
in the sun. I climb the stairs to Special Collections
where clear wood and white make Leonard French's
stained glass feel on the edge of being shushed.
My trolley rolls on wheels that never dream
of squeaking. Within the boxes' simple origami,
the folders slide against each other with the sound
of slipping between sheets in a five-star hotel.
I stack Antarctic journals into bright, geometric bergs

and turn each page softly, the paper clean and dry
as surgeon's skin. Knowledge is an odour,
acres of shelves stacked to the walls
with calm air sleeping in the spaces between.
A freshly unwrapped version of myself, I work solidly,
spine straight and more orderly than at my own desk.
When the librarian glances up
I tuck my ink-stained fingers away.

IV

I weave through a mess of runners and blossom
under unrolled bolts of sky and lake. Walking back
to the hotel, the Parliamentary Zone is green-neat,
missing only the drone of mower or bark of dog.
I know where I'm going. Adelaide is the map
tucked in my back pocket, folded against the grain.

Lost on the coast road

after Rowan Ricardo Phillips

I'm about to get this all wrong. This place,
so stacked with shacks and gin palaces
that I keep getting Middleton and Marion Bay
stuck together in my head, both flecked
and slapped with the Southern Ocean and its winds.
The windows are down and we let
the air overtake as Alistair's car carries us
like a metaphor that doesn't quite work.
The moon is fat with light
and floating in a sneeze of stars
so we crank back the seats and let
the cries of crickets replace conversation.
We've rambled ourselves to a standstill
and Bulkey wants food so we turn east
without a map, as though some Orient exists,
searching for something intangible yet substantial,
spiced with fiery accusations of its own,
the breezy tangle of stars and streetlights
finding us then letting us go.

The sound of the Anthropocene

Black Point, Yorke Peninsula

I've driven from a place of edges
and endings to this cold winter shore
where the line slicing water from sky
is nothing but softness. A bird blacks
a hole in the grey and the sea is so still
only gull legs and wing flap ripple the glass.
I leave footprints in the sand, mistakes the sea
will erase with no uncertainty, reminding me,
at last and again, why I'm in love with the wild.
The houses jostle, this beach the thin partition
between worlds, the deep ocean currents
and the tireless germination of human things.
I dig for the earth's elegant fierceness, this poem a fossil
pressed within the stratigraphy of my notebook.
A black and white dog escorts me to the Point.
Her place, not mine. A flock of egrets gaggles,
some flying out over the water, clapping wings
above low bellies. The dog brings me a sea rock,
drops it at my feet with a clatter of tooth on stone.
The sand is a welter of toe-prints, a crackly mosaic
of shell. Each step gives such a satisfying crunch.
Even though. Even though it is the sound
of the earth cracking beneath my weight.

The pleasure of getting nowhere

'I have nothing to say and I am saying it and that is poetry.'
—John Cage

Five seasons without rain. The cold south wind at our backs,
we walk the creek bed, stones chiming beneath our feet.
We are learning to walk the ancient way—quietly, shoulders loose,
skimming the earth until the soles of our feet have ears.

I see you and sense that you see me, your eyes
inland seas in the desert. We lean into conversations
clasping wine in hands that brush only once. It felt solid
but those words were just a flash flood through arid land,

our pasts layered deep below, millennia of strata laid down
and buckling from primeval tensions, our exposed surfaces
sculpted by eons of weather into this fleeting formation.
It's the archaeologist in me to want everything laid bare.

Now I'm back in my ordinary happiness and just like that
I've blown it, failing to grasp how easily words create silence.
But on clear nights I'll spin warm fictions from these spare stars,
my ears straining the quiet for your voice. Rain brushes my cheek.

Outside the polar tent

Ross Ice Shelf, Antarctica

My camera can't focus, everything's so close
and warm within our tent's citrus glow.
But outside, Mt Erebus is lost, wind and ice
now one thing and one thing beyond sight.
We hunker, our palms worshipping the Primus
as it labours solid through liquid into comfort
and steam. We are fragile as skin, our dusty
homes so distant it's as if we are astronauts
planting flags on a world so white and cold
we are breathing starlight. Beyond the ice,
beyond the currents straining through
the great nets of latitude, green vibrates
with heat and bugs, soil lying soft against
the hills and gullies of the earth's bones.
Are we colonists or pilgrims? All I know
is that we are a people of parkas and data,
wind-proof gloves and pink pee funnels,
clasping our fear and heat close
to the hot muscles of our hearts.
All I know is that we are a species
so hungry we could gnaw the stars
from the sky.

Envy and the Dunning Kruger Effect

I'm in the University Bar drinking wine
with one of my best friends. She's successful,
but she's been talking about her agent's
lack of interest for over an hour. I'm listening
but only to the edges of what she's saying
until she looks at her phone, squeals and throws
her arms around me. A publisher, just that minute,
said yes to her poetry anthology. The same guy
who has had my work for six months with no word.
I'm so jealous I can't tell the difference
between hating her and wanting to be her,
my whole being stripped to a trip-wire of want.
I hug her. Say I'm happy for her. But
it's a happiness that carries hunger inside it.
And while I'm smiling to cover that hollow,
a memory rises like a developing polaroid.

I'm on the Ganges, watching the pyres on the ghats,
the lights of Varanasi smeared across the water.
The air is clogged with oily smoke as the bodies burn
and the heat tightens the skin on my face and the backs
of my hands. Ash dusts my hair. The guide hands me
a tiny boat of leaves carrying a marigold and a candle,
tells me to ask the Mother Ganges for my heart's desire.
I set the little craft adrift, watch its light wobble
across the metallic water. *To be a great writer.*

I've read enough fairy tales to know I'm playing
with fire. There's always a twist. Greatness,
if it comes at all, will arrive once I'm dead.
Or if my words somehow survive the apocalypse,
fame will descend not from merit but luck,

like the Greek and Roman scrolls now deemed
classics when really, aren't they just the ragtag survivors
of the day Alexandria burned? Dunning Kruger
might have something to say about this moment,
hugging my friend outside the Barr-Smith Library—
my hubris in thinking myself her peer, blind
to my own incompetence. Surely, great writing
demands a lyrical 'show, don't tell' scene,
my jealous shame speaking its own language,
the version of myself I thought I inhabited
revealed as a husk. Greatness. I've begged for it.
But isn't the question what would I sacrifice?
I kiss my friend's cheek, look up at the night.
What I'm aiming for feels as far away as Orion,
as forgiveness. Maybe this is what it takes,
embers of envy fanned into flame. And the sacrifice?
Light splashes across my shoes. In the library
my crumpled pages are prayers rattling into air,
each line, each poem an offering of blood.

II

CHLOROPHYLL & CASEIN

poems from Sottochiesa, Val Taleggio, Italy

'My eyes were in my feet…'
Nan Shepherd, *The Living Mountain*

'The poets have been mysteriously silent on the subject of cheese.'
G.K. Chesterton

Pacing myself

I'm learning this place with my feet
my map of this valley sketched
with the rhythm of old knees.
I pack my bag for the day with water,
fruit and ten words of Italian then follow
my curiosity as it winds uphill,
a meadow pilgrimage accompanied
only by questions and this stingless sun.

My hope for this poem is a looped tale
with all the obligatory peaks and plains,
my body finding its way back to the start, weary,
grounded, with a touch of redemption thrown in.
I pass the cemetery early, so perhaps this trek
will be something other than a simple
metaphor for life, the sun-strewn valley more
than a place to hang my ignorance out to dry.

I climb into the woodland that hovers,
waiting to invade the vast beds of grass
that shine with burgled constellations.
Up past chiming cows and the reach of church bell
into shade that slides across my skin while insects
careen like electrons around fresh piles of dung.
My steps are a rosary, this body a prayer chanted
in panting breath, letting loose my airy molecules
to mingle with the sky standing so tall in the valley.

Even in shade layered upon green shade,
my sweat drips, tourist salt and water rudely
shouldering themselves into this private cycle.
Through Fraggio, where San Lorenzo sprouts

from the grasses, the ruins like tiny eruptions
of sandstone, the mountain's gizzards asserting
themselves amid the shallow chatter of grass
and woodland. And then the road. Pasture
stacked upon pasture under naked sun.
All I can hear are midday crickets, the chaotic
orchestra of cowbell and the awful rhythm
of my limp turning this trek into one long
iambic line all the way up to Cappo Foppa.

And then the turn, where poems and paths
should gather new strength, a surprise reveal,
the place you discover yourself a stranger
in your own story. But here there's no
single moment, just a slow amassing
of awareness that I'm lost, and so the turn
is literal, even if I say *volte*, in the hope
that Italian might lend some romance.

You would think it's all downhill from here
but I'm turned around in Grasso until I find
the tiny track to Ca' Corviglio with its tumbling
water and Madonna, where the words
for trespasser and dogs stretches my Italian
to a dozen. I shuffle back into Sottochiesa, knees
creaking under the bells of San Giovanni Battista
and some empty-handed thunder, while summer
keeps falling and falling with nothing to slacken it.

Summer storm and leaf litter

Sometimes air feels most
like itself just before rain.
    Clouds surrender to gravity
    and when rain writes itself
    in grey italics, even the stones
    read. Leaf mould promises sweet rot
              and mushrooms, deep in these
              green shadows where I hide
              from the plasma flash and rumble.
    Nothing changes quicker than light.
    All movement is now water
    and down, the insects and birds
    quiet. I don't know these trees
              or who their ancestors were
              but we are all standing together
              in the rain and I'm tracing us
      back through the aeons to a place
      before we drifted apart, to the life
      from whom we are all descended
the bacterium, the monocotyledon,
the cosmic dust the world spins out
into all its making and unmaking—
      back, back to when all possible life
              was dissolved into one.

Credo

There are a million ways to know something. This is one of them.
I'm walking this valley but seeing it with words.
Like taking a photograph then writing myself into the frame.
The world makes the lines and the lines make the world.
I'm in the empathy business. I want to knock you into another skin,
another scale, another set of worries and come to love the estrangement.
Don't we all reach for wisdom? Sometimes I like feeling for a keyhole
in a door that opens onto something so much bigger than myself.
I want you to feel the trauma of the present, these words my hands
shoving humanity off its invisible throne.
The house is crumbling. The contractors are hopeless.
Let it fall. Everything comes apart. Everything reaches blindly for another form.
Blood and thunder. Starlight and grass. Enzymes and happiness.
All dissolved into something more. Something good.

How to build the Alps

It begins with stone.
Heat. Pressure. Formation.
Each layer spreading its fresh sheet
over the one below. Foliation is such
an organic word for orogeny.
This was back before flowers.
When words seemed tiny.
Moss. Fern. Spore.
Only fifty million years until
things grew to picture-book size.
Plateosaurus. Ticinosuchus. Ceresiosaurus
Then the extinction. The one before this. Before now.
Bivalves, gastropods and brachiopods don't fare so well.
Diversion. Deformation. Laurasia and Gondwana part ways.
Waters obey physics and Tethys, the Mother of Oceans is born.
Orogenesis. Compression. The Alps have nowhere to go but up.
It sounds sudden, but all the while, flowers are working
the kinks out of pollination. Dinosaurs grow
feathers and a love of wind. Around
here, when you start tunnelling, you
find more than grottos of red limestone
or quarries of black shale. Dig deep enough
and you'll find the scaffold of everything.
The pieces that fit together into something
complicated and profound. Fragments
of colour and shape that you can slowly,
painstakingly, with trial and luck,
piece together into water, into sky,
into grass. Memory and desire.
History and perspective.
Ourselves.

13 thoughts on Alpine pasture

1. Grasses are the delicate conduits through which the earth feeds itself to the sky.
2. The pasture speaks a hundred languages, its dictionaries running to seed with thousands of words for light, microbe and weather.
3. To the grasshopper it is a metropolis of stem and space, creating its own climate.
4. Pastures are deceptive. Beneath wild skin, they hide ancient bones.
5. The valley is a museum preserving artisanal collaborations of ruminant and human.
6. Nothing exists without threat. The woodland, that patient coloniser, lies in wait to stretch itself across these vast beds of grass shining with a harvest of galaxies.
7. Time is counted by various clocks. Summer days pass to the ticking of grass seeds, cowbells ring out the passage of seasons. The mountains sleep through the aeons, occasionally twitching in their dreams.
8. These fields look made for romantics, but they are the homeland of pragmatists.
9. Rancière says that looking is not the same as knowing. A single field can hold a gaze longer than life.
10. I want to hear the stories of the soil's dark realms, but I do not speak that tongue.
11. I have heard the high pastures called *man-made*, but the stones hold up the sky.
12. Cow and human alike bend to the will of the grass.
13. And all the while, the pastures get on with their steady work spinning cellulose from light.

Pasture ecology

after Tracy K. Smith 'The Everlasting Self'

The pasture
weathers the flood of light
shedding pollen in every direction—
a seasonal responsibility:
sprouted, unfurled, flowered, then
eaten, absorbed. Like life
from centuries past or dung
a cow has left across the field.

The flood of light eaten, then absorbed.
Across the field, a cow has left life
or dung in every direction,
shedding pollen from centuries past.
Then eaten—a seasonal responsibility.
In every direction the flood of light.

The flood of light weathers
the shedding pollen: sprouted, unfurled, flowered
like life or dung
in every direction. A seasonal
responsibility, like a cow
from centuries past.

The pasture, eaten.
The flood of light sprouted,
unfurled, flowered, absorbed.
Or dung like life across the field
in every direction. Sprouted,
absorbed, like life or dung.
The pasture from centuries past,
a seasonal responsibility—eaten.

The inside of a cow

Inside the belly of a cow is untouched
by the clean face of the moon.
We are not so different, she and I. Complex and
contingent, we float between subject and object.
No longer just one, we are arrays of bodies,
landscapes for the species travelling with us.
Vibrant matter, we carry worlds within worlds,
our boundaries porous, the microscopic other
redefining our grammar. Our singular is plural.

It is dark. It's dense and industrious. This rumen
is a metropolis for microbes—bacteria, protozoa
and fungi all cohabiting, a collective enterprise
fermenting the green of the fields, cracking
fibres into short chains. Fatty acids. Proteins.
It takes time and a return ticket. Rumination –
such a perfect word for considering the world.

The honeycomb of the reticulum. The leaves
of the omasum. There's an organic theme to life
down here in the dark. Water is filtered away
and finally, the abomasum - the 'true stomach'
in the mouths of omnivores and creatures not
used to digestion as meditation. Enzymes
and acid. The final stage. What is created?
Energy. Gas. Milk for the calf, or, if the calf
is stolen, for the human. Microbes sustain her,
feed her, that vast raft of inner life the fuel
keeping her metabolism alight. Carbon dioxide.
Methane. Shit. The microbes give, then
they take away. Nothing is free.

Her blood is rich, caseins clinked into chains.
Rushing through ever narrowing vessels,
they squeeze from blood to the lumen,
tributaries gathering flow until milk pools
in the pink lake of the udder. Lumen, the light
within, clean face of her internal moon.
She is the sunlit grass and the dark metropolis,
the individual and the populace. My plural self
is a desert island. She is a whole ambling world.

How to make Taleggio cheese

1. Put down your load. You've lugged its awkwardness so far, knees and back weathering every step up this mountain trail, pace matched to the herd's chiming amble.
2. Once you've straightened and stretched, tend to your herd. You know their names. Watch their joy at finding themselves on this elevated island of sweetness.
3. Scratch your dog behind the ears. She's done well.
4. If you can spare a minute among your tasks between the *baita* and the herd, take it. The summer light is long but can't last forever. Fill yourself with this air. See how the mountains layer themselves against the jagged horizon? These distances are yours for the summer.
5. And now – the milking. Everyone knows their place. Forehead leaned into flank, your fingers pull and press, a soft accordion thrumming tender ballads.
6. Take the milk inside and stoke the fire. The night will have teeth.
7. Pour the milk into the cauldron. It's cow-warm, so the only heat you have to maintain is your own.
8. Add the rennet. You knew the calf from whose gut it came and remember the rasp of its tongue seeking salt from your skin. When you were a child, your heart was fresh and soft as Agri di Valtorta but the years have cured it. Now it is as hard as Pecorino with a rind that is thick but not yet bitter.
9. Give it some time. Drink coffee.
10. When you can draw your grandfather's Bergamasco blade through the milk and see the cut, slice a grid through the curd. Pick up your brass bowl.
11. Scoop the bowl through the curd, wrists circling in a delicate churn. You can't even remember how old you were when your wrists stopped tiring from this. Keep scooping until the curds float like ghostly pebbles in a golden pond of whey.
12. Fetch the cheese cloth from your saddle bags. Line the buckets. The lengths fit perfectly, aged to sepia as if you've used them to strain tea.

13. With the brass bowl, scoop the curds into the buckets. When they are full, lift the cloth, curds hanging like fat puddings.
14. Let the whey drain with a noise like you make outside after a long night of grappa and tales. Keep it. Nothing is wasted. Pour some into the dog's bowl. When she looks at you with those eyes, ice-blue and mud-brown, add a little curd.
15. Place the curd-fat cloth inside the wooden mold on its thin bed of straws. Four bags, a perfect square. Leave it. More will drain.
16. Eat dinner. Feed the fire. The winds are falling off the mountain. Polenta with donkey sauce sits heavy in your belly.
17. Turn the cheeses over. Gently. Then pour some grappa. Sing. The nights up here are long. Keep the *baita* warm. Turn the cheeses. Again. Again. Then, when you settle down to sleep, let them settle too. Everything finds its best self under its own weight.
18. When you wake, tend to your cows. This cheese must grow used to waiting.
19. Prepare a brine with water, salt and a splash of vinegar. One by one, float the flat squares in the brine and turn. Let them dry.
20. Everything ages in its own way. But first, let it rest. This shouldn't be rushed. Let the cows lick the salt from your hands.
21. Send the cheese down the mountain. It's ready for the next stage. A dry, wrinkled skin. Wish it well. You will meet again.

Marking time

In the valley's creases, where water and air
fall towards a rumoured sea, I find the markers.
Incised stones lean over streams and troughs,
stating their mossy claims. S.V and S.M—
they assert ancient boundaries from the time
Da Vinci was in Milan painting *The Last Supper*
and the Bellinis brought colour to Venice.
Those city-states knew a thing or two
about power and the value of trade.
Owning the grasses that fattened the cows
that produced the milk for the most famous
cheese in the land? That was something worth
fighting for. And they did. Ancient stracchino,
taleggio and the grandfather of gorgonzola,
that delectable blue and double-curded strachitunt.
The Duke of Milan loved his cave-cured cheese
so much he demanded a quarter of a tonne
before his unfortunate conviction for necromancy.
Gorgonzola had celebrity clout. Beethoven adored it.
George IV had both swagger and excellent taste in cheese.
History brims with those unlaced by the things they love.
I cross the border onto Milanese turf. The Brembana
Valley rolls towards Lake Como, the wind is busy
elsewhere and it's so still I can hear every green thing
breathing. Vedeseta fits perfectly together,
the air crisp as a fresh sheet and all is at peace
between the belltowers in this valley where
the grass is wholesome and cheese can spark wars.

Poem digesting a poem

I face the mountain as if it is the north
of my body's compass and climb, walking
my boots and jeans dry. A golden eagle
circles in the light that slices its way
to Lake Como and I taste yesterday's storm
on the air. The noxious and the delicious
nod their heads as I pass but I still can't
tell one from another, like I'm travelling
with a map of the wrong place.
The cows hold their wisdom modestly.

An hour uphill and I'm zigzagging for shade.
Clover, dandelion and the wild spinach I ate
in ravioli my first night here. Blackberry
out of sync with my garden at home.
Past Bonetto, with its Original Browns,
Swiss Browns and a protective mother
who stamps and flaps her ears with only
a thin orange tape between us. My legs
know only incline and stubbornness, pulling
this body with its hefty crowd of strangers—
microbes, bacteria, the atoms of the long
dead and those I've yet to meet. Together
we stride through dappled forest, airy leaves
so green it seems the chlorophyll is singing.

                                          we, the unseen

                    know ourselves through other eyes

                                                so much

                    action in the dark
the crystalline palaces

                    of minerals
                                        bacteria's fractal multiverse
we are the subterranean
                            the swing and tug of the moon
            the gut of a cow
                                    her microbial oceans
            the vast clan of protozoa
                        dark tides wash
                                    from rumen to abomasum
you call us simple
                                    but when is energy artless?
                in the shadowed places
            we know death
                    by its true name
                                    part of becoming is unbecoming
we are all
                        fragments
                                    of the whole

If prayer is a focused wish, the old gods
were listening. The stream was as sudden
as a something secret breaking the surface.
I thanked the oreads, my bottle now full
of cool sweetness. And again the climb,
past cowless pastures with their tumbled
baite and craze-bottomed ponds, a scooter,
a table-tennis net, an umbrella dead
but neatly folded. I see my destination,
where the tree-line can't quite reach,
Chiesa di Maria Santissima Madre tucked
into the bed of the high plain. Thunder roils
across the green spine, indigo cumulus
piled in its wake. I scurry, hoping the thin
shelter of beech and birch will deflect
any random firing. The air is three dimensional
with seed-drift, striped flies hovering as I flee

through forest, the fern carpet twitching
with unseen lives. I am utterly alone, yet
completely surrounded, so warm in the suit
of my skin that the tiny lives in my sweat
proliferate wildly. The sun is tilting towards
the lake, the world swarming in every direction.
An ermine gambols from the ferns and freezes.
We meet eyes, its chestnut alertness
allowing me no defence against
its scrutiny. It stands, vest gleaming,
then without a backward glance, slips back
into its day with a liquid grace, while the valley
keeps glowing with the gentle smoulder of summer.

Reality check

Halfway between magma and starlight, this place is far from simple, everything the colour of joy and envy. Hera Lindsay Bird would call me an emotionally articulate, meadow-frequenting, piece of shit dumb-ass. I watch like a stray cat in the night, *tapetum lucidum* flashing. My night-vision is keen but I can't tell how much data reflects back, not even passing the retina. I don't see that the kids have moved out, the houses squatting damp and shuttered. There's a brisk trade in '*vendesi*' signs. Nomads drive trucks and trailbikes. Apprentices are front-page news. Ponds are dry and cows drink from bathtubs scummed with the dead. Mowers are in vogue but prosthetics for maimed wildlife are yet to catch on. Forests are making a comeback. Cows chew grain over grass. The cheese has moved down into dairies while plants clamber up to escape the heat. Species creep. Climate crisis. And who knows what's happening with the snow? It all looks bucolic, these roads up the mountain like glossy eco-porn. The marketing people forgot the rainbow. How much change can the planet take, anyway? I don't know my chestnut from my beech, but some things are clear. The forest gives way to the fence. Vapor trails crosshatch the blue. The world is torn. Every morning, the chaffinches are singing before I open my eyes.

How to make Taleggio in the 21st century

1. It's a gamble who will arrive first—you, the truck of raw milk sloshing with the morning's offerings, or the light.
2. Take a moment to drink in the day. Feel the dawn's warmth on your skin and the moisture in each inhalation. This is not mere pleasure. Temperature, humidity. Before you even step through the door you sense how the milk will behave, the curd's performance.
3. Loop yourself into the white plastic apron, cup your hair in the tissue cap and slide your feet into the pallid rubber boots. You are the colour of milk, curd hardened into muscle. The tiled room of white and steel is stainless; the only splash of colour that blue stripe of tiles above your head.
4. Glance at it throughout the day. Remind yourself of sky.
5. Fill Vat 1 with raw milk and flick the stirrer into motion. The clamour of day begins, a mechanical orchestra with no intermission.
6. Tip the plastic jug of rennet into the vat. The liquid is the colour of pale gold. It's been many years since you thought about baby goats. Look at the blue stripe.
7. Thirty minutes passes quickly. There is always something to be scrubbed, to be turned, to be stacked.
8. Cup some curd in your hand. You can tell when it's perfect, the silkiness gathered sweetly on your palm.
9. It's time for the first cut. Slice the long blade through the curd, slice and slice until the surface is crossed-hatched like the street-plan of a New World city.
10. Wait five minutes. Then sweep the long cheese harp through the curds. Craft currents and whirlpools.
11. Pick up your stainless-steel dish and stroke its edge through the vat. Again, again, again.
12. Alternate instruments until the curds are soft brash ice in the polar sea of curd.
13. Suction the whey from the vat and let it flow into the metal trough and away. This will be butter in its next life. Nothing is wasted. They say this. You suspect it's marketing.

14. Scoop the curds into the grid of gleaming baskets on their bed of plastic straws.
15. Let them drain. Already, the tiles are awash. Water and whey pool around your feet.
16. Put aside some curd for the strachitunt curd-blend tomorrow, the round, corded hoops stacked and waiting.
17. You don't need a timer, the knowledge deeper than bone. If it was written, it would say turn the dripping baskets after thirty minutes. You turn them when they need to be turned.
18. Do this five more times between now and tomorrow. Deftly. Instinctively. Let the curds sink until they assume their true form.
19. Pick up the stamp, the grid of four circles fitting perfectly on the base of the cheese, the bottom right bearing the mirrored numeral 42.
20. Stamp the cheeses. Emboss them with the mark of your heritage, your expertise, your home. At the precise moment of contact they become more than cheese, the weight of tradition and symbol escaping the scales.
21. Repeat steps 5 to 15 throughout the day until the shelves are full and the vats empty, everything hosed, scrubbed and dripping.
22. Stack the cheeses and let them sit, marinating in their smell, the sweet curd overpowered by the volume of whey, the whole building redolent with saccharine sourness.
23. Let them rest for two days, keeping you company while you work, the cheeses the only life sitting still in this place.
24. Then send them on their way. You won't see them age, tucked away in the cold humidity of a cement cave.
25. For the next two months they will mature then be shipped away, perhaps to the south or perhaps across an ocean.
26. You will stay here.

End-stage pastoral

Water and time change everything. Like all complicated stories,
this has both running through it. Above and underground.
Deposition and erosion. Traditions and modernity.
Migration. The picturesque and the pragmatic.
The Bergamini still lead their herds to the high pastures.
On foot or by truck. Or they don't. The fields are still auctioned
for the summer, the land parcelled by the cows it can feed.
Cheese is made. Or it's not. It's eaten in the valley. And shipped
beyond the equator. The line and the circle. One can be bent
into the other. The cows keep the forests at bay
but isn't everything marching up the mountain?
Dry-stone walls crumble. The doors to the *baite* rot.
Motorbikes zip summer milk down to the creamery.
Shutters stay closed. *Vendesi* signs bloom like geraniums.
The church-bells sound the hours. Rain falls. There is grass.
Milk. Butter and cheese. UNESCO and DOP. Heartbreak
and indifference. Beautiful weeds. Arduous customs.
Species loss. Conspiracy theories. Hay and pasture.
Curds and whey. Glaciers retreat. Forests follow.
Money moves to the city. People follow.
Stones tumble into pebbles. Years tumble into days. The line
can't quite touch its toes. Water and time change everything.
Like every complicated story, this has both running through it.
The Salzana flows into the Enna. The Salzana flows into the Enna.

The flipside of the postcard

I love the word *pristine*,   the naïve impossibility of it,
        all of us vulnerable, impure and trying to make do
    in a world where every postcard   has its grubby underside.
Nothing is untouched.   The bright air is packed with pollen
desperate for the sticky clutches of stigma.   The soil
        beneath our feet is a microbial orgy in the dark.   Even
        our atmosphere is just air the ozone is done with.
What seems to me a paradise is a cage to someone else,
    pulled between a salary and tradition,   obligation heavy
as a stone in every pocket,   desperation burning marrow-de
    The wolves no longer howl on the mountain.   Marmots
        chitter at hikers.   Tail-lights and horns on the winding road,
    more traffic flowing out than in.   In the *baite*, the black
weight
        of roof presses down until walls buckle,   a terminal swoon.
Everything feels the pressure.   It's all on the move.   Sometimes
I feel like I'm just here to take inventory.   To witness the world's
  slide to wherever the hell we're going. I hear the word pristine and laugh.
        But there's no humour in it,   like an undertaker chuckling
    politely
at a graveside joke as everyone
            tries

            to keep a grip.

It takes a mountain to raise a cheese

You want answers, so immediately I'm in a panicked state.
What is a regenerative economy, anyway? I'm a writer. My time
is spent exploring on foot, trying to see things differently.
Like the way the *piode* is a jigsaw from below but from above is a roof.
That's a bit simplistic. Trying to give you answers is making me careless,
the way I get back to the room, pull off my boots and sling my bra
not even looking to see where it falls. Some think nature is all about sex
but I'm leaning in another direction. I'm missing the moonlight.
All this walking has me in bed with the sun, weighing the valley's life
and trying to piece it together with words. You want me to show my thinking
but resisting the seduction of witness and metaphor is not easy to overcome.
It's as if you've offered the finest single malt whiskey but refused me the ice.
I'm trying to be critical and speculative but I'm just grinding out the syllables,
constructing poems from form, allusion and a well-thumbed catalogue of words.
I'm great at questions, seeing how problems connect and replicate.
But critical speculation? I'm a dog yapping at unseen dangers. I can't say
what should happen here, all the possibilities clamouring. I can't tell prank calls
from those with something important to say. The word on the street
is it's better to ignore what you see. Go with what you perceive.
My bedroom window is black with possibility.
What can I offer? I walk. I watch. I make poetry.
If only I was more original, walking around like a pregnant woman
confident in the form of her creation, her offspring welcome among us.
I'm not used to being so beyond my depth.
Here, all the surfaces are peeled away, lack of faith in myself
laid bare in these echoing lines. I scratch pen on pages to start fires.
The answers are needed, the world staring down its own destruction
and here I sit twiddling around with rhythm and the fall of a word.
Beyond my window, the darkness resolves into birdsong and branches.
Grass will grow. Cheese will be eaten. These futures are not empty yet.
But I'm not so deaf that I can't hear this valley whimper.
It's just that I've no particular claim to wisdom—

only the ability to watch, witness and fill with the pities
of someone gifted in seeing backwards. It's a leash,
the tug of it jerking my head as I peer into the night's potential
beyond the green-sided mountains

                          all the way to the glaciers
                          all the way to the wolf's return.

III

CONTACT TRACING

'One touch of nature makes the whole world kin.'
Shakespeare, *Troilus and Cressida*

'Life is a shipwreck, but we must not forget to sing in the lifeboats.'
Voltaire, *Candide*

Social distance

1. #couchlyf

The Great Storm of 2020 rolled out indoors.
Before now, news seemed careless.
We could take it or leave it. On TV
I see people go to bars, catch elevators,
kiss. It's so casual. *Twelfth floor, please.*
See you. And I feel as if I'm watching
something decadent from a golden age—
Scott & Zelda splashing through fountains
drunk and glittering. I took it for granted.
The full supermarket shelves. The freedom to jump
in the car on a whim. Go to work.
Hug my friends. Rub my eyes without
thinking of respirators, hand sanitiser
and the collapse of global markets.

Anxiety roils like my last pot of ramen
but the bad weather is all in my head.
The sky is a clean blue bowl. We drink beer,
drag the couch outside and watch the waves
fling themselves on the granites in either
grief or joy. It's just one more uncertainty.
I call Mum, her voice enfolded in smoke.
No veggie seedlings at the garden centre.
Dad's grumpy. No, she doesn't need anything.
It's just good to hear your voice. We watch
the syrup of sunset thicken, then head inside
to curl up in last week's unmade bed, lips
stumbling to mouth words we have yet to invent
as we try to teach ourselves new ways to pray.

2.   Zeno's Paradox in lockdown

Through the honeyed slide of hours
I practice the art of arrangement,
composing the room into this day's
still life. The books. The lamps.
The empty vase, just so. The treacled
gradient of light and cool subtraction
of dusk. Time sliced so thin it stops.

They say binaries are dead. Perhaps
that's true, in everything but code.
Yet here I sit, trapped between
life and death, every viscous instant
sliding slow as Zeno's Paradox, waiting
for all the infinite divisions between
one and zero to clot into days.

The window tenderly cups its garden.
This poem, even in all its black and
white weightlessness, is at heart
just one more still life unsure of its true
nature—particle or wave or some
unknown in-between—as I inch along
this immeasurable path towards zero.

3. The death of walking

Last year in that boot-shaped land, life was all about feet.
Size eleven, bunions, footprints like continents. The delight
of strolling from the sun-strewn Spanish Steps to the alleys
of Aventino, my stride threaded with stress after scattering
self-respect in the gutter outside the Baths of Caracalla.

Trundling my suitcase to the foot of the Alps, at last and again
it was all about feet. Everyday sunshine and grasslands boiling
with colour and cowbells. At home, to walk alone was an act
of greed. Here, I swung my arms, free of guilt and leash and
strode those hills, my limp sounding the valleys to a solo beat.

Today, these ugg boots whiff of wet fur but the couch is bare.
My heart slugs indigo inside my ribs. Time is thinner here.
A place where even soft things break. There's no reason to walk.
The pace of my days no longer thumps to tailbeat or wet-nosed
pleas for scent-snuffle or messages left on bark. The leash hangs
by the door. The outside is a fable I once believed. Days pass
coated in burrs. Boots gather dust and the fruit bowl grows fur.
Weak light slides in but the beds of sun lie empty. This ache
is fractal, hollowness blooming boundless hollows, ears tuned
for the jingle of tags that does not come. World-worn, I tuck
away my feet. The empty couch stretches itself, quiet and cold.

4. Self-portrait reflected in the TV

The first thing you'll notice is hair.
The kitchen looms like Satan
in the background. Silver shapes
curl beside me. A wolf and a greyhound.
A kelpie, a ridgeback, a tortoiseshell cat.
One living, four ghosts. It's dark as childhood,
hermetic as a ship trapped in a bottle.
You can't tell my jacket is blood-red
in the screen's liquid black.

There are books. Pens. A vase of beauty
some call weeds. Reading glasses
with a crooked right arm. Puppy-chewed,
a detail mentioned in the interpretive panel.
If you knew me, you'd be surprised
the tv is off, expecting my reflection
as a double exposure across *Black Widow*
or a Wes Anderson film. The notebook is open.
The light in the room is blue wren song,
the soundtrack a podcast by Natalie Haynes.

Dim as an engine room at night
the room's vibrancy is a secret.
Even my face is grey-scale.
This is no Nerudan 'Self-portrait as an
animal of light'. Ideally, there'd be
symbolism artfully strewn about.
A few *memento mori*. A globe.
A skull. Significantly selected titles.
Instead, there's my diary and a 'to do' list.
There *is* a stuffed raven. On the walls,
forgeries. Rivera. Kahlo. Preston.

You can't see the Van Gogh. You can't
see the construction, stroke by stroke,
of something that doesn't say anything new.
The whole idea is to instil doubt.
Is this an original? A forgery of a forgery?
In the dark mirror, the spectre shifts,
crossing her legs. Her pen scrawls across the page.
But you can't read the words.

5. *The Lady of Shalott* in 2020

The grand architecture of the world
has shrunk to my fence-line
and places I love call out in thin voices
as if locked in distant rooms.

My days unspool in a single stretch
of light, stained only by the ordinary
miracles of cloud track, voice mote
and the thump and drag of blood.

My mind is the bathroom mirror
after a shower. It's not death or curse
or loneliness I fear. It's forgetting who I am.
A woman in love with the wild.

Each day I knot words onto pages, trace
the path of the planet by the cedar's shadow,
study the syntax of birds. Curling toes in the grass,
I dream the history of this place layering down

to its dark core—molten and churning.
In the old world, enchanted by light and quiet,
I was not in love with people. Yet here I am, half-sick
of shadows. The night rides in. The stars hang,

keeping their distance. I gaze out at the world
through the glass but see nothing. No passing knight.
No bearded meteor. No broad stream complaining
in its banks. Just my reflection crack'd from side to side.

These unprecedented times

Above the masks, our eyes are windows of elevator music.
We cruise the supermarket canals,
filling trolleys with turmeric and chew toys.
It's the end of a meme, the news cycle our bread and testosterone.
The best way to create a welcoming home
is to decorate with barbed wire. Hermit chic. It's all the anxiety.
We're not in Adelaide anymore, Toto.
I'm running a tight shipwreck.
Sourdough, rubbish sculpture and recreating
the Old Masters with serviettes and tablecloths.
We've all taken a deep dive down the relevance hole.
There's no better feeling than staring at a wall with closed eyes.
Every town is a museum.
This is nature, red in reception desk and management.
Can't we all just speak to your supervisor?
All for one, one for the conspiracy theory.
Don't get your knickers in a parachute,
there's plenty more crises in the sea.
If it's too hot, get out of the government.
This is what humans do—when life gives you a virus,
storm the Capitol. It's the law of the knuckle sandwich out here.
Another day, another axe to grind. Opposites exploit.
Please. Let's all just take a deep border closure.
Don't cry over the best medicine. Forgive and vaccinate.
Then wipe the slate with sanitiser.

The Attic of Anxiety

It's always there, gripping the brow of the house.
Push open the trapdoor. It squeals like a horror flick.
The space is close and shadow-crammed. The rafters
demand a hunch. You'll need a torch. The beam
will spotlight one item at a time with startling focus.
There'll be so many things you'll recognise. Masks.
Your old softball glove. Your coaching whistle.
That stack of journals you really should've burned.
Furniture from your first marriage shrouded like ghosts.
That whirring sound is an old projector flicking memories
against the far wall. Faces of boys you hurt. That time
you dropped the relay baton. Every drunken conversation
of the past three decades. In front of the screen
is a battered chesterfield. An art deco side table holds
a cup of black coffee. Sit down. The coffee is steaming.
You'll find the leather perfectly moulded to your shape.

Bandwidth

After Destiny Birdsong

I know you're busy, but
You work from home, so
Thank you for your kind donation. Now
Keeping 1.5 metres apart, please
I think the government should
Thank you for your submission. Unfortunately
You don't have kids, so
You saw the latest figures? How
If you are feeling unwell or have been interstate, please
I love your hair, is it
The direct debit for your scheduled payment was
When you go past the shops can
Unfortunately, your application was
Your concession card is
Are you Mrs or Ms
Are you a *medical* doctor
Are you going to
Are you free on
When do you think you'll
The current fire danger warning is
Have you checked in
The total comes to
Can you enter your
I'm sorry but
Have you
Can you
Are you
You

Room 8, Rose Court

Dad curls in his chair—ammonite or foetal—
I can't tell. Only that every visit
he's twisted a little tighter.
You're too old for those shoes, he spits
then gums the straw in his lemonade
like a newborn greedy for the nipple.
The doctor said not to worry about the sugar.
The cancer will take him before diabetes.
He dozes. Mum and I chat softly, laugh.
His eyes snap open. *Cold.* I close the window.
Pain. Mum presses the button. Peter comes
with morphine. Dad thanks him, asks
the flavour of today's juice. Mum heats his soup
and when I kneel to tuck his blanket around him
I can see the loose flesh gathered
into the legs of his diaper. *Bloody static.*
He throws his headphones at her.
Mum slides them back over his ears
then tugs lambswool slippers onto feet
so swollen they are pudgy, like a baby
before walking moulds them to the bones.
He curls in his chair, king of this cloudless
one-room nation where time is no longer
linear but circles him—waiting for an opening.
He doesn't say goodbye.

The Great Conjunction

I'm stooped in my driveway, eye to the scope
watching Jupiter and Saturn align in the sky
as mosquitoes orbit like moons. This year
only the planets refused to veer off course.
For almost fifty loops of the sun, Dad circled
the same house, same wife, but died alone
in a strange bed. Six months in a home.
He never left that room. Mum allowed at his side
for just one hour of every Earth's spin. Each time
I saw him, he tilted further off his axis, curled
and surly in the arms of a chair that didn't know his shape.
He died on the equinox. I didn't cry. I took notes
sitting on the loungeroom floor, as my family
sifted photos, trying to ignore his empty space.
Even standing in that tiny room beside the chapel.
His hair was all wrong. Swept back, not combed
across his forehead. Waxen skin, his frame still bent.
Left temple smooshed against the side of the casket,
one dark eyebrow flicked up on the white satin.
He was shorter. Calmer. Polo shirt and track suit pants.
His uniform. Even at other people's funerals.
In a suit he'd be a stranger. Liver-spotted hands
clutched his Crows scarf as if he felt the chill.
Scented candles and the strange smell of solicitude.
Rosewood and a brass crucifix with dying Christ.
The chapel door creaked. My brother, grief-eyed.
My notebook burned in the dark of my bag.
It came to me when I was at the lectern.
We all mourned a different man. This year
all we could rely on were the solstices, equinoxes,
our homemade gravity. The rest whirled off track
so fast we didn't even get the chance to divine

the mess the stars promised. The wood ducks
with their spring then summer clutch of young.
The candle burning for my brindled hound.
And in highest branches of the pine, the heron
keened and keened her wild and lonely cry.

The day you left

In memory of Alison Flett

The sun didn't come up this morning, Adelaide gifting you one last taste of Scotland. Walking to the Botanic Gardens, everything is silvered and soft, revealing only what's right in front of me while the distance tucks its secrets away. I'm twenty minutes early. They are twenty minutes late. Any other day, irritation. But this morning, I wander in the fog, thinking of you, the stillness broken only by the carols of magpies. Lines are brewing, but I'm too ashamed to be caught turning your last minutes into a poem. But you? You'd be thinking poetry. And later, you'd bring it to our group, something with atoms or *umwelt* and a fox peering out through the black bramble of lines and we'd all be floored by what was going on in your head while we were debating where to get coffee. There'll be no later. A jogger runs past in full make-up, her body a perfect expression of youth and vitality and I think 'wait until middle age' then the gut punch of knowing that's all you got. Years ago, Heather gave us both a card with an old woman in a red polka dot bikini and wild sunglasses reading a book as she sat in a deck chair planted in the sea. *This will be us when we're old!* And now you are lying in your bed, surrounded by husband, kids and the boxed faces of your family on a screen. We stand in a tree-draped gazebo, holding each other, one of us a crying face cupped in an iphone as the moment ticks by. The candle-flame wobbles, then lives on. I can't stop thinking something should happen. The flame guttering to smoke. Foxes streaking around the cup rim in an amber blur. We wander away for coffee and the sun burns through as we pass our grief between us. Walking through the city, it's a new world. Everything is you but the tense has changed. The yellow of that knitted headband you loved. Looping my leather backpack over both shoulders will now be Alison-style. Every Parklands cyclist was you standing on the pedals as you pushed off towards home. I pass two Christians with their pamphlets and Laminex display of smiling white faces and I want to kick it to shards. I want to scream in their faces what sort of god? Driving home in my hatchback, a ladybird flies in. It creeps through the dust of the dash. Trying to save it, I knock it into the footwell where it's lost among the sand, bakery bags and keep cups. But no—here it is—shiny spotted wings the exact orange and black of that mod dress I gave you when you first got that pixie cut. And you looked so freaking beautiful at that poetry reading at Heather's as we sipped afternoon light from our wineglasses. I remember it was getting dark and we were sitting together under the low heaven of party lights as a poet read from her iphone. She'd lost her place and was scrolling and scrolling and we grinned at each other as the pause stretched beyond awkward into some uncharted space. And I can't remember if the light hitting your cheekbones was from the moon or the strings of tiny stars, but I'll hold that moment forever—the dark thickening but you somehow still shining as the poet kept scrolling and scrolling and scrolling because she couldn't find the words.

Field notes on rain

I take my demons for a run.
Try to lose them in the grey air.
The road knows its way
between the stringybarks.
The invisible world made solid
drums against my hood.

The fat patter brings back
that first night squatting inside
the ruin that would become home.
Windows just holes for wind,
the dark shot with volts. And company?
Those spiders weaving dreams above me.

By the waterfall, it eases.
A soft grey drift, like a good cry
in the morning leaves you
teetering on the brink all day.
The landscape draws itself
then erases into blank distance.

The scent of wet eucalypt
heavy as a fallen curtain.
Four subspecies of rain.
I keep on, hood-blinkered
through all these hills and roads
I carry along the dark bitumen.

Stand

After Ada Limón

Two years I've lived as if in a cul-de-sac,
a flat sun bathing me in cold blue glare,
my griefs orbiting like silt-faced moons.
Yet in dreams, I soar with bar-tailed godwits,
guided by gut and stars over the vast blue curve.
Manna gum, I see you, pale bark a clean flame
licking the night. Please, tall one, tell me
how to relish stasis. How do you stand,
rooted deep in the loamdark as life sparks past,
the years a doppler rush of flicker and change
under a twirling sky. I try to feel my way
into your body, a hard thing dressed in weather,
needing nothing but to cradle all these quick lives.
This year, my autumnal equinox swung past,
decay etching my skin and honeycombing bone.
What's it like for aging to be an act of creation?
Your hollows house rosellas, koalas wedged
between cloud and grass. Wattle-bird, lorikeet,
honey-eater all feast on waves of flowerfroth,
ants sipping sweetness beneath hangnail bark.
Human lives race towards you and away
by foot, then cart, then car—for you each day
a mere falling mote of light. What's it like
to exist like an open door, arms wide?
Even as the eucalypt ocean shrinks to islands
you stand—a pacifist in the heart of battle.
When you find yourself living in a graveyard
packed with monuments to loss, please,
old one, can you teach me how not to fall?

Acknowledgements

Many thanks to Australian Poetry, Illaria Mazzoleni, and NAHR (Nature Art Habitat Residency) for the incredible opportunity to spend a month in the village of Sottochiesa at the foot of the Alps in Italy, writing the poems that would become the heart of this book.

Sincere thanks to the Australian Society of Authors and the ASA Mentorship Program.

I was incredibly lucky to be awarded Brook Emery's mentorship and guidance. Thank you so much, Brook. Your insight, vision and generosity were invaluable.

Poems in this collection have been previously published (sometimes in slightly different form) in *Abridged* (Ireland), *Antipodes (USA)*, *Australian Poetry Anthology 2018, 2020 & 2021*, *Australian Poetry Journal*, *Foam:e*, *Grieve Anthology 2020*, *Magma Poetry* (UK), *Mapping the Human City: Poems of Adelaide Anthology*, *Mascara, Meanjin, Meniscus, Not Very Quiet, Plumwood Mountain Vol 6 #2 & Vol 8 #1*, *Poetry d'Amour Anthology 2020*, *Pure Slush, Raining Poetry, Red Room Poetry*, *Red Room Poetry 20th Anniversary Anthology, Saltbush Review, Science Write Now*, *Social Alternatives, Stilts Journal, Stylus Lit, The Result Is What You See Today: Poems About Running* (UK), *Transnational Literature, Westerly, Wonderground* and *Verity La*.

'The pleasure of getting nowhere' won the 2020 Poetry D'Amour Prize.

Sequences of these poems were shortlisted for the Newcastle Poetry Prize in 2021 & 2023 and highly commended in the Charles Rischbeith Jury Poetry Prize in 2019 & 2020.

This manuscript (previously titled *chlorophyll & casein*) was shortlisted for the Unpublished Manuscript Prize in the 2022 Adelaide Festival Literary Awards.

I am so lucky to be surrounded by friends who are also brilliant writers. Heather Taylor Johnson, Katherine Tamiko, Rebekah Clarkson, Bronwyn Lovell, Narelle Hill and Shaine Melrose—thank you, lovely friends. Your presence refills my creative well.

Alison Flett—you are deeply missed.

To the Meanies: Alison Flett, Heather Taylor Johnson, Julie Cebulla (JayVee!), Mike Hopkins (Father Mike), Jennifer Liston, and Louise Nicholas—thank you for the laughter, feedback and outrageously libellous meeting minutes scribbled on serviettes - our degenerate band will never be replicated on the Mean Streets of Adelaide.

My sincere thanks to Shane Strange and editor extraordinaire Penelope Layland. I'm forever grateful to you both, and everyone at Recent Work Press, for your all your hard work and support.

And finally, as always, my deepest thanks to Andrew Noble—first reader, tireless listener and staunchest champion of poetry (even after being repeatedly woken by midnight notetaking). You are my bedrock.

About the Author

Rachael Mead is a South Australian novelist and poet. She's the author of the novels *The Application of Pressure* (Affirm Press 2020) and *The Art of Breaking Ice* (Affirm Press 2023) as well as four collections of poetry. She holds a PhD in Creative Writing from the University of Adelaide and was awarded the Barbara Hanrahan Fellowship at the Adelaide Festival Awards for Literature in 2022. She is also co-host of Adelaide's Dog-Eared Readings.

www.ingramcontent.com/pod-product-compliance
Ingram Content Group Australia Pty Ltd
76 Discovery Rd, Dandenong South VIC 3175, AU
AUHW020639050325
407891AU00002B/16

9 780645 973273